LET'S EXPLORE THE MOON

SPEEDY
PUBLISHING

Speedy Publishing LLC
40 E. Main St. #1156
Newark, DE 19711
www.speedypublishing.com

The Moon served as light in the night, but what do you know about the MOON? Here are the fun facts you need to know about it.

Water was discovered on the moon in November 2009. That was identified as Lunar water, the water that is present on the Moon. Liquid water cannot persist at the Moon's surface, and water vapour is decomposed by sunlight, with hydrogen quickly lost to outer space.

The Moon's orbit around the Earth is a slightly squashed circle called an ellipse.

The Moon has quakes. These are caused by the gravitational pull of the Earth.

The Moon is very hot during the day but very cold at night. The average surface temperature of the Moon is 107 degrees Celsius during the day and -153 degrees Celsius at night.

The Crescent appearance of the moon occur when it is being illuminated by the Sun, you can often see the shadow of the rest of the Moon. This is caused by reflection of sunlight from the Earth

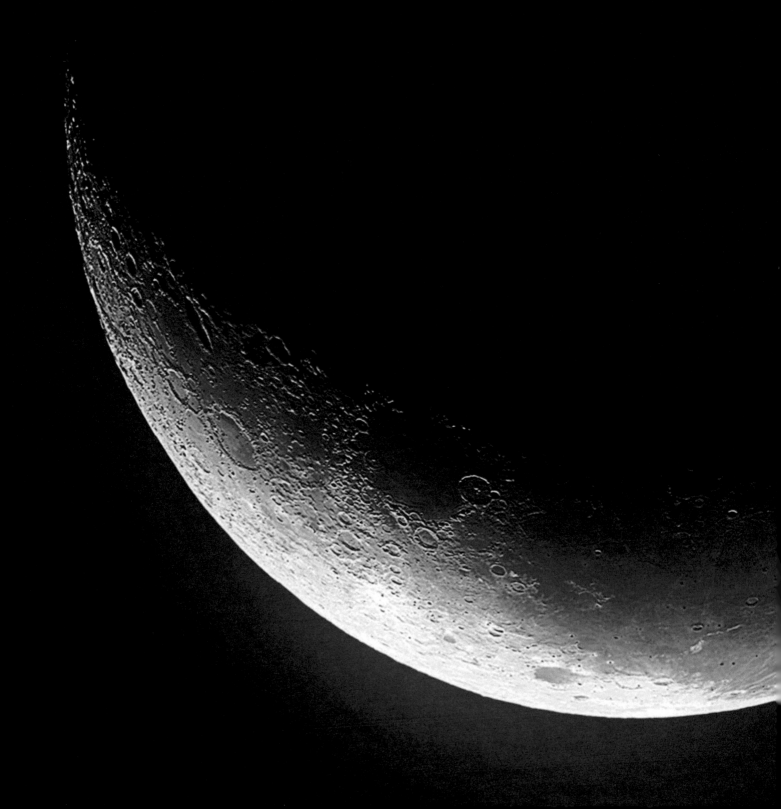

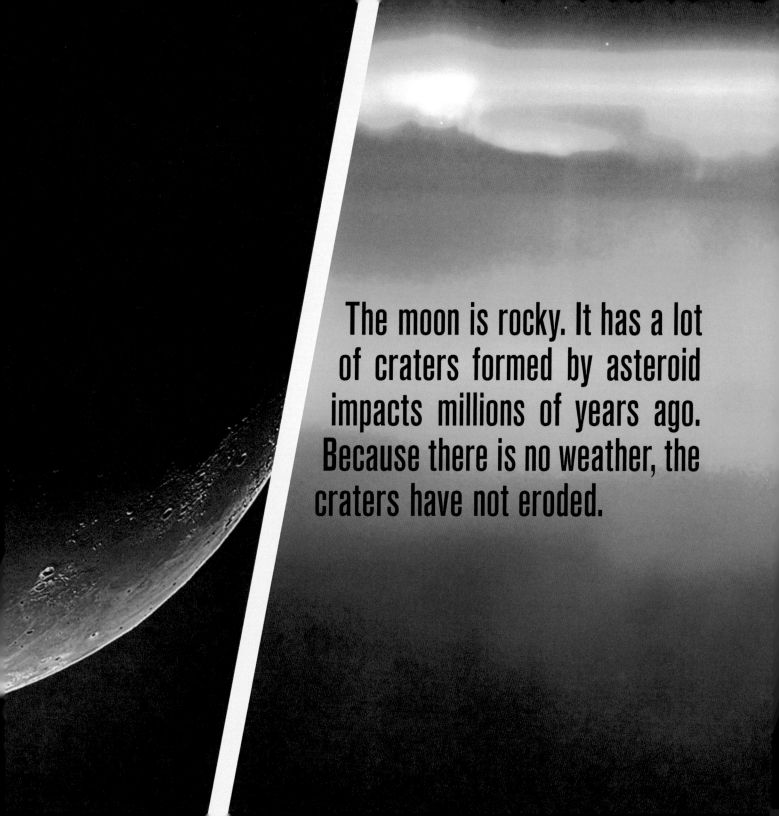

The moon is rocky. It has a lot of craters formed by asteroid impacts millions of years ago. Because there is no weather, the craters have not eroded.

The Earth's tides are largely caused by the gravitational pull of the Moon.

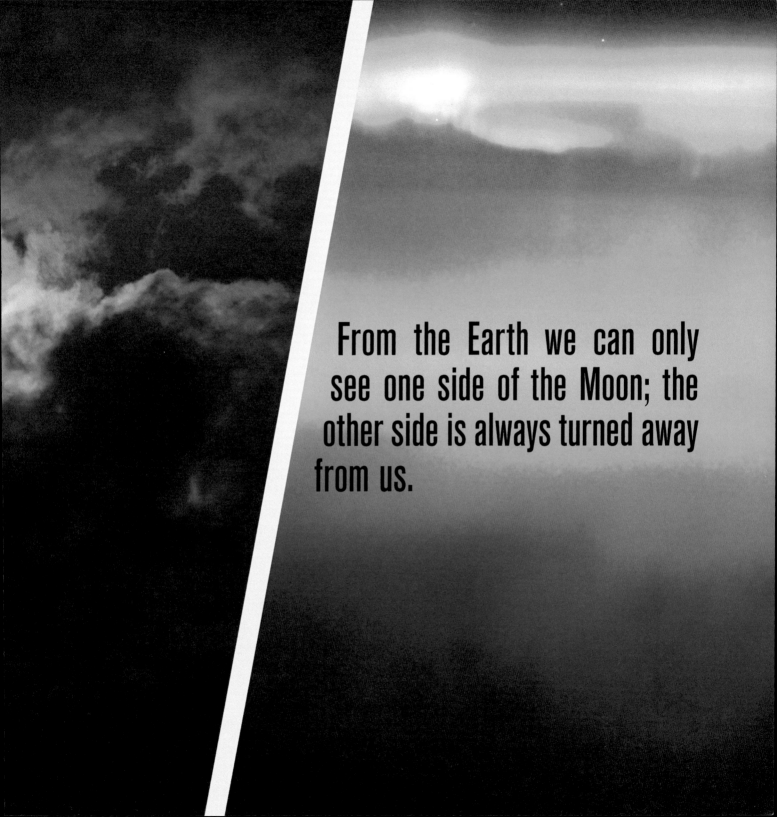

From the Earth we can only see one side of the Moon; the other side is always turned away from us.

The Moon is 4.5 billion years old. The age of the moon was identified with the help of "geologic clock".

The phases of the Moon are: New Moon, Crescent, First Quarter, Waxing Gibbous, Full Moon, Waning Gibbous, Last Quarter, Crescent, New Moon

The Moon is Earth's only natural satellite. It is one of the largest natural satellites in the Solar System

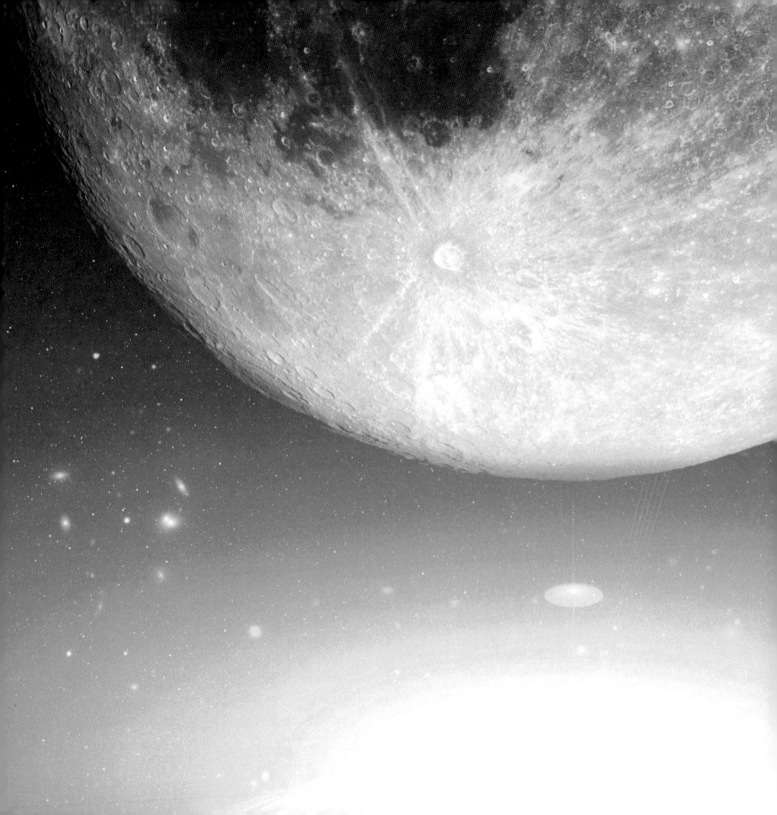

The Moon is about 250,000 miles (384,400 kilometres) from Earth. It will take 130 days if you travel it by car (referring to the distance only), 13 hours using rockets and 1.52 sec by light speed.

The Moon is in synchronous rotation with Earth meaning the same side is always facing the Earth.

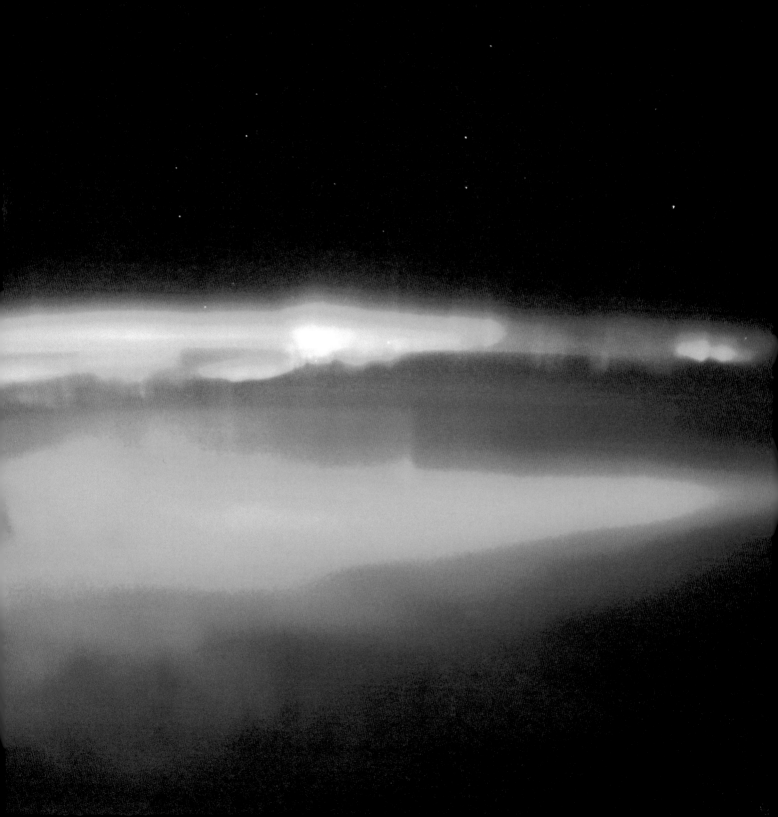

The Moon has no atmosphere. This means no sound can be heard on the Moon, and the sky always appears black.

Made in the USA
Las Vegas, NV
01 May 2022

48254389R00021